IMMIGRATION:

THE ESTABLISHMENT

OF THE NEW SELF

JOSIEL PEREZ-HERNANDEZ

ISBN: 9781697688221

Book Cover Designer: Richie Molina
Formatting Designer:Hui Chen

"Man is capable of changing the world for the better if possible, and of changing himself for the better if necessary."

---Viktor Frankl

Contents

Author's Note

This is a nonfiction book, which is a collection of some of my experiences, stories, and strategies that have been guiding me through the eight years that I have been in the United States. I hope this book will serve as a guide for immigrants who are professional or not through their path to become part of " mainstream society". The purpose of this book is to guide, inspire, and empower immigrants who were professionals in their "home country" and desire to transform themselves in a new society. This work does not cover stories accounts. It reveals the author's journey.

I am thankful to many who helped make this book a reality. I am thankful to God for letting me share my stories with you. My family in Cuba encouraged me to write this book. My parents, Jose A and Elena; my sister, Mileidys, and my brother, Isbel. To my wonderful niece and nephews, Diamelys, Aaron, Isuel, and Osvel. I hope this book inspires them to continue focusing on their goals. My Grandpa, Miguel Perez, who taught me the importance of having music in our lives. My uncle, Andres, who encouraged me to be the best version of myself, especially in my professional music career. My cousins, Quirino, Evia, Demirel, Dariel, Jose Miguel, and Yoania. My extended family in Cuba and in the U.S. Chantal Tademy, Nieves, Maria Elena, Aldo, Mercy, Milagro, Yalil Guer-ra, Maria C. Cacarnakis, Jose Ferrero Arrieta, Mercedes Rodriguez, Aldo Martinez, Ya-cel Varela Garcia, Mario & Annette Atencio, Lester R, Arnaldo Acosta, Alli Hawks, My-ron Oakes, Hector, Cathy Zubia, Danny, Brian De la Fe, Yosmel Montejo, Ivan Llanes, Gloria Weil Herrera, Ann Reynolds, Luis Conte, Mariano Morales, and Ruth Silva. Thank you for paving the way, believing in my dreams, and having faith in me.

This book would not have been possible without the unconditional encouragement of Irene rhodes. Irene has been motivating me to write this book and to be honest about my own perspectives. I want to thank Anastasia for being a magnificent writing tutor and advising me through this process. Many thanks to a dedicated team of professors--Dr. Sandra Stauffer, Dr. Margaret Schmidt, Dr. Jill Sullivan, Dr. Jason D. Thompson, Dr Evan Tobias, Dr. Paul DeCastro, and Dr. Ndindi Kitonga.

Prologue

Josiel Perez-Hernandez is currently working on his Ph.D. in Music Education at Arizona State University. Prior, he earned two Master's Degree--Film Scoring and Master of Arts in Teaching. In 2010, he was awarded with a Bachelor's Degree in Music Performance at the Instituto Superior de Arte in Havana, Cuba. Since 2007, he has been a professional musician touring in Europe, The Caribbean, Asi, The U.S., and Canada and also performing in Jazz and world music festivals. Additionally, he was part of the cast for the movie CHEF 2015 and in 2017 he received a Certificate of Appreciation from The City of Los Angeles. Josiel Perez-Hernandez lives in Tempe and has been serving as an adjunct faculty at Paradise Community College since 2017. In the future, he would like to help more immigrant communities to achieve their dreams.
Visit www.josielperez.com.

Introduction

Early in the morning, I enjoy the silence and intimacy between me and my cup of tea. Early in the morning, my writing comes alive and my soul is pure. Early in the morning, my memories appear as if they were ghosts and I begin to write this book.

This book is intended for new immigrants who come to the United States (U.S.) to pursue their education and success. Each immigrant's experience has their own definition of metamorphosis. Metamorphosis: meta "after" and morphe "form"; a Greek word meaning transformation. Several researches define metamorphosis as an "integrative concept" related to "developmental" biology, ecology, life history evolution, physiology, cell biology, and conservation biology and as part of adapting to a new environment or "landscape" (Bishop, Erezyilmaz, Flatt, Georgiou, Hadfield, Heyland, & Reitzel, 2006). An immigrant's metamorphosis is their process of adapting and transforming the self in a new country, becoming a butterfly from a chrysalis. Mahalingam (2013), states that "immigrants are exposed to dual worldviews, cultural practices, and beliefs" (p. 2). In my experience, metamorphosis has been a process of imitation, adaptation, experiencing displacement, relentless attitude, practicing gratitude, and agency in those dual worlds, cultural practices, and beliefs. Entering into a new culture with a different set of values, traditions and priorities requires a dose of boldness and humility. Understanding that I am a stranger in a new culture made me observe and imitate the way nationals think and behave.

As pertaining to sets of values, U.S. nationals protect their privacy, which is one of their closest values. For example, when meeting someone unknown, one should not ask personal questions. For many nationals, this means crossing a personal boundary. Time is needed for people to open up to new individuals. Further, children are taught to be independent and to be in charge of their own decisions and life.

In addition, learning the secrets of dating another person differs between countries. Mistakes might be made, but trying to know another person may take several dates by spending money and energy into getting to know the other person and maybe, at the end, they are not interested.

The host culture has its own laws, culture, and behaviors that have been developed over hundreds of years. The U.S. is so rich in resources, traditions, education, and culture that people are still uncertain of the definition of what it is like to be an American. For new immigrants, it is challenging to keep up with understanding the way different communities live and interact in the U.S. This country is constantly changing, exchanging and borrowing ideas from other countries around the globe. Therefore, it is your duty to find your own definition of what is like being in the U.S. and to know how to negotiate this definition and identity within a new society.

Being an immigrant in the U.S. represents a perpetual negotiation between culture, tradition, religion, and language between "the home culture" and "host culture". Most of the time, it is an endeavor to try "to make sense of the host culture" and explain what life is like back in "the home culture" to nationals (Mahalingam, 2013). Therefore, it is your decision with who you want to associate with and on what level you embrace the "host culture."

Each chapter focuses on particular challenges and opportunities that I have had while living in the U.S. The challenges and obstacles I had to face and overcome motivated me to achieve my goals. The opportunities of living in a new country has allowed me to find my own path to success. I believe each person has their own definition of success. I have been fortunate to be able to share my music with various cultures, people, and generations. I truly value waking up and being able to practice and share my life's passion. In my case, this is performing and teaching music. In the U.S., I was able to accomplish my personal dreams, such as having my own musical group and recording my music album called "Conga Buena" in collaboration with renowned music artists such as Kamasi Washington, Luis Conti, Jimmy Branly, and Dennis Chambers. In 2017, I completed my second Master's degree; I had the opportunity to join the Paradise Valley Community College's faculty. These challenges reflect my particular struggles while being an immigrant and the opportunity to start a new life in the U.S. has allowed me to obtain a perspective of what it is like to be an American. The objective is to understand the journey of an immigrant and to have the ability to expand one's limits and push the bar of what is possible.

My story began in 2010 when I finished my Bachelor's degree in music in Havana, Cuba. That same year, I had the opportunity to join a prestigious Latin Jazz band in Cuba, "Orlando, Maraca Valle's band." I toured in Europe, Asia, and part of the U.S.

In 2011, I arrived in the U.S. while touring with a band from Cuba. At that time, the relationship between both countries were starting to improve because of the President Obama Administration. I dreamed that I would continue my professional musical career and education in this country, so I decided to stay without telling my family in Cuba because if the Cuban government knew about this decision, the possibility to stay in the U.S. will be difficult because an artist works for the government and are not allowed to pursue independent contracts.

During this period, I learned that it is important to trust in the immigration journey and let your consistent work ethic and discipline pave the way to your success. I believe that having a spiritual guide, such as a religious entity, cultural identity, or mindfulness, is crucial for the moments when we are not in control of our path. A support system such as friends, family, pets, etc. Around you will affect your decisions, successes, and lifestyle. As part of a support system, one should maintain close relationships with friends that value and appreciate you, not because of your assets, but because of the way you make them feel. These individuals should be an integral part of your close network of friends.

Furthermore, this process of staying to establish my life and career in the U.S. has helped me in the transition to improve my life, the people around me, and my family back home. I heard many stories from new immigrants who are very successful professionals, such as artists, engineers, doctors, and lawyers, in their countries of origin and came to this country only to end up working in low paying jobs and delaying their dreams.

I hope my own experiences will guide and enlighten you on your way towards reaching your dreams. Once you learn to start creating your short and long-term plans, your ability to reach your goals and dreams will change in positive ways. If you find yourself thinking, "I'm never going to make it," this is the message that you are sending your brain. In my experience, visualization is an effective technique to combat negative thoughts, which is about positively envisioning where you see yourself five years from now. In my journey to fit into this society, I had to learn about assimilation, imitating how successful people think and act or "fitting-in", and co-switching, adapting to the environment where I am. Co-switching, or "changing codes", is defined as changing the "language behavioral" and" dialect" (Nilep, 2006). Further, co-switching is either consciously or unconsciously a part of a new immigrants social behavior and used as a way to adapt and fit into the "mainstream" society. Over time, I noticed a change in my thinking and began seeing the results. Some of those results are the ability to observe and adapt to different work environments without losing my own identity. Therefore, if you feel that another successful immigrant is doing better than you, it's OK. Establishing one's self in a new society takes time; learning a new language, working while studying in uncomfortable places, getting your finances together, and educating your family back home about the process of becoming a new citizen in a new country is a part of the journey. This book will support you and guide you; I know you are closer to your goals than you were yesterday.

The reason I wrote this book is so you can have a resource that I did not have. Instead of reinventing yourself, you have a resource to read on your journey to fit into a new society and pursue opportunities. I know everybody has a different experience when coming to a new country. However, if you find yourself lost, discouraged, and hopeless, perhaps my experiences will help you find the way to your goals and success. The idea is not to work hard and postpone your dreams but to balance your time between making a living and pursuing your dream. In addition, most immigrants, who are professionals, in the beginning are so deeply focused on the process that they forget to write about their experiences, so they can help other new incoming immigrants. My mission is to leave a written legacy for thousands of new immigrants and immigrants who are professionals who desire to continue their careers in the U.S. In these times of social, political, and economic uncertainty for many immigrants, this book is a great resource to continue planning, visualizing, and striving for a better future.

The Overview

This book is about some of the immigrants who are professionals in their country of origin struggles and possible strategies to overcome these struggles. This book provides insights for immigrants to assimilate more smoothly into American society. I share my story as it is something that most immigrants share in common. Specifically, our ongoing struggles and success in this country that presents many challenges, unique opportunities, and a means to succeed. It is my personal struggles and desire to share my perspective with others.

Mattoo, Neagu & Ozden (2005) state that current professional immigrants with education in their "home countries are ending up in jobs that make little use of their education" (p. 256). Sometimes, because of the lack of information and connections, many immigrants who are professionals do not know where to send their titles, certification, and transcripts so they can get certified to work in the U.S. When I arrived in the U.S., I desired to continue my profession in this country. It took me two years to know someone that could guide me through this process. I highly recommend this resource: www.a2zeval.com. This independent evaluation company, located in Davis, California, offers an international credential evaluation to the U.S. equivalency. I believe this Me: An Immigrant's Metamorphosis is a good resource for those immigrants who are professionals wishing to continue their career in the U.S. However, no matter how well we do in a new country, immigrants at some point would like to be reunited with their relatives, not only as part of their economic success but also personal fulfillment.

Most immigrants hope to reunite with their family in their " host country", but this process can take between five and ten years. Becoming a citizen and establishing financial security in the U.S. is crucial towards accomplishing this goal. Gathering the finances and any relatives' paperwork can be a stressful and exhausting endeavor. During the process of arranging my parents paperwork, I struggled with finding a professional translation services company that could translate birth certificates. Luckily, after a long search, I was able to learn about this company called The Arizona Language Center (www.arizonalanguagecenter.com). Through this company, I was able to translate my birth certificate from Spanish to English. Moreover, make sure you know people in your community who might be a resource for you. If you just arrived to the United States as a refugee or are seeking family immigration services or further education in English as a second language education, I highly recommend you get information at www.friendlyhouse.org. Since the 1920s, Friendly House has been providing services to immigrant communities. In general, ASK A LOT OF QUESTIONS! Do not get discouraged because there are a lot of resources out there who want immigrants to succeed.

Although there are other notable books about immigrants in the U.S., Enriques' Journey, which is the story of a boy's dangerous odyssey to reunite with his mother, written by Sonia Nazario, provides a clear description of how his mother was forced to leave their homeland to provide for her family by moving the U.S. Due to these circumstances, Enrique traveled to the U.S. and faced various obstacles in order to find his mother. "The Newcomers, Finding Refuge, Friendship and Hope in America," by Helen Thorpe captures the stories of various refugee teenagers from various parts of the globe and details their challenges, such as adaptation to life in a developed country and dealing with adolescent issues while limited in their ability to speak the English language. Most books I have come across are good resources to comprehend the current issues and challenges of immigrants in the U.S., however it is also important to discuss possible solutions to combat the ongoing challenges that most immigrants face. Therefore, I hope this book will encourage and motivate you in your own journey to not only to be successful in the U.S., but to also contribute to other people's success. Our intention is to build a community that facilitates and provides resources for those immigrants that are in the process of arriving or who have just arrived in the U.S. to then transition smoothly and collectively be a part of the community to be mentors to others in need.

Univision Arizona Ft. Gina Santiago

The Immigration Journey

When I was growing up, my mom used to say, "There is always someone in worse condition than you." Until one day I said yes in response, "But there are people doing better than us." The 90's was a difficult time in Cuba. We were in the middle of the embargo and we were struggling to access the primary necessities such as soap, toilet paper, toothpaste, and food. In some places, the dollar was banned and the Cuban peso did not have any value at the time. I remember my parents making a dish of corn flour for lunch and dinner for months. For breakfast, sugar water with lemon was popular in school and at home. Eventually, I refused to eat corn flour and sugar water with lemon. The only problem with that was that there was no other food to eat. Still today, I cannot stand a dish of corn flour.

Upon my arrival in the U.S., although I was excited that I had the opportunity to work and send money to my family in Cuba, I was missing the loud music coming from my neighbors' home, the hot and humid days swimming in the river close to home, especially Sundays when most people were resting and getting ready to work on Monday. My soul was screaming for some Cuban loud music and the indescribable tropical smell of rice, beans, fried plantains, and roast pork. Music and homemade food are part of Cuban traditions. Most of the time, when visiting a friend or a family member, they usually share a homemade dish with you and a topic of conversation related to an artist or popular song. I boldly state that Cuba is one of the few countries where Arts are appreciated and valued. Artists are as respected as doctors and lawyers. As a music artist, I notice the difference between being an artist in Cuba and in the U.S. In the U.S. when you are an artist, some people expect that you have another profession. According to Steiner & Schneider (2013), "artists earn less than they would with the same qualifications in other professions" (p.226).

My dream was to become a world renowned artist in the U.S.. Although I still hold this dream close to my heart, I realize that for me to invest in my artistry, I have to continue pursuing my education and place this dream on the back-burner in order to focus on establishing myself financially. Being a music artist in the U.S. requires having financial means to produce an album to promote myself while working to establish a name for myself. Essentially, establishing a name for myself requires promotion and getting my music out there. Therefore, touring is an effective way of working towards my goal.

In 2011, I was touring around 28 cities in the U.S. During our tour break I went to

New Mexico with a few Cuban, Cuban American and Puerto Rican friends. That was the first time I had experienced freedom because I did not have someone monitoring my every move that was appointed by our government to oversee our travels in the U.S. In that moment, I realized that I had to stay. Although it was the biggest decision in my life, upon returning to Los Angeles to continue with my tour, I spoke with my uncle who was part of our band about my decision. My uncle did not agree with my decision but gracefully accepted my decision. My uncle was from a different generation. He did not understand the importance of expanding my horizons as a musician. My uncle and I approached our boss about my decision in which my boss responded that he would retain the majority of my earnings while on tour, therefore resulting with only $120 in my pocket. I came across an old acquaintance who was part of my support network and who had a friend that was an attorney. With the assistance of my support network and the immigration attorney, it afforded my smooth transition with regards to living in the US. The moment my fellow musicians departed the U.S., I started to experience displacement knowing I was not proficient in the English language with no mode of transportation, let alone the ability to drive a vehicle. The moment when my colleagues departed, I felt isolated and lost. However, deep down I knew it was the right decision to make. I knew my decision would break my parents heart until today I realized that they were not ready for my decision however, my spiritual guidance and my vision allowed me to see beyond the pain that I and my family were experiencing. This made me more driven to change my current mindset to be more optimistic. I believe my mother did a significant job in teaching my siblings and me the importance of being grateful.

There is no existence of a perfect journey, only your own that you are about to start. I need to admit that migrating to a new country conjures mixed feelings between being frightened, hopeful and unsure of what destiny has prepared for you. The first one that comes to my mind is the feeling of displacement. Overcoming the sense of displacement was one of the biggest challenges I've had. Internalizing this as a new home takes time. I manage to visit my "home country" twice a year. Although lately, I am aware of where I consider home. It only takes the right amount of experiences to displace me and make me change the definition of my home. Angelika Bammer, in her book "Displacements: Cultural identities in question", describes the term "the memory of a struggle", which relates with cultural and geographical displacement that new immigrants experience upon arriving in the U.S. (1994).

Where am I? How do I fit into this society? How do I see myself five years from now? Those questions have the possibility to clear your mind of any mixed feelings and guide you to your purpose. It does not matter where you are in your life at this moment, as long as you plan and be aware that the decisions you make will impact your success in a new country. Each person has their own story and path to walk. So, do not compare yourself with someone born in the U.S. because it takes time and investment to be part of the "mainstream culture."

Trust the Process

The final project is the object that needs the process to be closer to perfection, not the other way around. Some individuals focus on the final product. I get it, the final product is the outcome and the evidence of a process filled with learning and endurance. Personally, I find myself struggling with being patient during the process. I find that having patience and placing trust in the process is where the quality of our product will afford me tremendous future possibilities. My fear is that during the process of seeking a high quality product, I find myself procrastinating on the purpose and become easily distracted.

Touring in US 2011

A Born-Again Person

Born-again is the conscious action of walking again. People often ask me, "Josiel, what is it like to start a new life in a new country? How long have you been in the states? Is your family here or are you by yourself?" Every time I address these questions, I explain to people that each experience is different and everybody has their own born-again story. Some folks migrate with some advantages. They learned or earned an English degree before coming to the U.S. Definitely, this allows them to speak, write, and communicate fluently in English. Therefore, this advantage opens many doors. Some migrants come from wealthy families, which provides an economic foundation as a security to invest and do business without struggling to find a job. In this chapter, I compare the idea of starting a new life in a new country with the idea of being born-again. For newborns, imitation, modeled gestures, and emotional expressions are part of their early stages of social development (Suddendorf, Oostenbroek, Nielsen & Slaughter, 2012). For some, immigrants who are professionals in "plural societies", psychological, sociocultural, and economic factors determine the process and success of adapting to a culture, which is "the process of becoming part of the 'mainstream' culture" (Berry, 1997).

I consider myself a learner. Being curious about different ideas and seeking knowledge as a way of educating myself has been and continues to be the best thing that has happened in my life. Education provides me not only an opportunity to learn the language, expand my knowledge, and build a career but also the privilege to meet great colleagues and friends who have helped shape my personality and way of thinking. Some of my best friends are more than simply friends, they are a part of my support system.

In fact, I come from a working-class family that values the arts and have taught me the importance of improving ourselves through education in order to improve the overall society. My family was not affluent, but they had a wealth of values, such as treating everyone with respect and dignity. Also, the importance of understanding where you are and where you are going. Those values that I learned as a child have been guiding and influencing my decisions. They are imprinted into your memory, so in crucial moments you have choices and are not obligated to follow other peoples' misguidance. My mother would say, "That we live the life in the way we think." Usually people who think about a healthy way of living will visualize the process that they will take to achieve their goals. I believe her statement rings true because you sometimes live with what you can afford, then it is your decision to live accordingly or beyond your possibilities. As immigrants, sometimes we feel tempted to live life the way the folks from the "mainstream society" would. Unfortunately, this idea overlooks the point that it took them years and generations to build their wealth. Therefore, agreeing or not, they set the standards and we will be foolish if we attempt to compare ourselves with them.

In my home, my dad was the main breadwinner while my mom was the thinker who would execute the vision for us individually to succeed in life while fortifying the family unit. It takes time and white hair to understand our parent's wisdom and to value the sacrifices they made for us. My mom worked in all kinds of jobs in order to sustain our family. My dad did not like to miss one day of work. Sometimes I saw my dad sick and he still went to work. My mom would say that even though we did not have a lot of money, we have the basic necessities, such as food and clothing.

I compare the idea of staying and starting a new life in the U.S. as part of being born again. Getting to know your new neighborhood and neighbors, work environment, co-workers or looking for a religion or intellectual community takes time and a willingness to embrace new cultures, traditions, and lifestyles. Three events influenced me reflect about the importance of being aware and understanding the "host culture".

First, if you plan to visit a friend, co-worker or family member in my home country, it is fine to show up without previous notification. However, this might be inappropriate because sometimes you may find yourself in an unpleasant situation, such as private family issues. Second, I had been in the U.S. for a few days. I started calling some folks from Cuba who were living in the state after 10:00 p.m. without realizing the differences between time of day or night and how important the sleeping schedule is for nationals. Third, Cuban talk is typically loud, especially when listening to loud Cuban music until midnight. I recall when I lived in an apartment community and the leasing contract said no loud music after 11:00 p.m. I felt disappointed and frustrated because my loud Cuban music was the only thing that reminded me of the island.

However, this experience and being an immigrant taught me the importance of understanding and respecting other cultures, traditions, and ways of life. Be aware of the society you live in and create your own way of life based on your values without following the "mainstream society" trends.

Change Your Mentality

If it were for the betterment of myself and my loved ones, I would prefer to pay the price of changing my mentality. We are in this life temporarily. We cannot afford to be narrow-minded and egocentric. This life allows one to learn and explore other people's perspectives. Personally, I cannot describe how much I have learned over the years while living in this complex, yet amazing country. Driven by the fear of uncertainty to pay the bills, house, car, and food, many new immigrants usually focus on working to make a living rather than understanding that the situation in which they are in is only temporary. As an immigrant coming from a third world country, it takes an average of five to ten years to establish oneself. This time might vary depending on whom you interact with, especially your support system. From my experiences, choosing to network around highly successful nationals has helped to understand the lifestyle in a new country shifting my mindset. Unfortunately, although we would like to continue sharing our culture and traditions with folks from our own "homeland," we find that some are still attached to their old way of thinking. The support systems you keep around you, family and friends will determine your success or failure in the process of getting established in the society. I surrounded myself with a support system and individuals who were a positive influence in my life that serve as a foundation for me to accomplish the goal that I have set for myself in the U.S. "A positive mentality can build a relentless attitude on how you connect with different events in your life. Overcome health issues and cope with stress" (Scheier & Carver 1993).

These supports can guide and encourage positive growth and change, such as learning a new language. Learning English for me was not a matter of learning a language but a survival skill that I needed to master. Some of my national friends sometimes state that they would love to be fluent in Spanish or another language. I often reply that it is a necessity, only necessity makes you find the courage and motivation to master another language. This is personal and not a hobby. From my own experiences, I have discovered that those who are not fluent in speaking English have limited job opportunities. Most job opportunities were graveyard shifts for those who spoke English as a second language. Another disadvantage to this was the fact that they received minimum wage, which could not afford a basic standard of living and thus resulting in having multiple jobs and less quality time spent with their families. Despite how my grammar, pronunciation, and accent were, I proudly continued speaking in English. Some

American folks might say, "I would like to speak another language" but, for me it is not enough to speak another language; it is about surviving and pursuing my career, business, and profession. I even joined the Toastmasters organization at my University. My favorite part was table topics. Real valor is required to create a story in five seconds and present it in front of people who are evaluating your speaking fluency.

To understand one's own mentality, one must first understand where you currently are and where you want to go. One way in working towards changing my mentality is about giving. I did this by supporting my family financially and, despite my struggles, I continued to focus on paying it forward because I am blessed myself. Understanding my investment in education while working and living with limitations, I continued to maintain a grasp of the bigger picture and simultaneously accepting delayed gratification.

Furthermore, I had to first understand who I am. I was born in Cuba and as a Cuban, we are very opinionated. Stereotypes are a trap! However, if you meet a Cuban, they always have an opinion about many topics, whether they know them or not. This is why I had to adapt my way of thinking in order to listen before I give my opinion. It is easy to get caught up in "this is me" and "who I am", and it is important to remember that we bring our own culture, customs, and ways of living from our own country. In other words, we might think about "am I imposing my own way of thinking." Is this correct? I would rather try to understand others perspectives and has proven to be beneficial in learning about others. Also, this helps me find what we share in common despite our experiences and cultural differences.

I remember in the beginning when I arrived in the country, I was texting my friends, some of them add smiley faces in the text and I did not understand why. Therefore, I had to learn what the message was behind this way of communication, such as using "!" as a way to communicate excitement. Also, the new generations start a text with "hey"; I was initially unaware that this meant "hi". People from different generations communicate differently, which I am not familiar with. Therefore, immigrants not only have to learn a new language but also the messages within the language. The question is, how much should I change? Another example is that the tradition in Cuba is saying Good Morning to others. In the U.S., this is not a tradition that is regularly seen. This is one difference between ways of thinking and interacting with others. I remember in the beginning when I had my first job, my co-workers were unpacking and eating their lunch without interacting with me. People in this country prefer the company of friends or familiar others rather than interacting with strangers. In Cuba, especially in rural areas, people treat unknown others with regard and acceptance, they are eager to serve and guide where you need to go. This is why it is important as a new immigrant to know who you are and understand how much you might change. It is challenging to be current about your country's culture and trends. Every time I visit my " home country", I find that there is a new cultural trend and way of thinking in society. This creates distance between me and my own culture due to the fast cultural changes.

Be Adaptable

It is up to you to live the different chapters in your life or die still writing the first one. Some people are afraid of risks because they have some degree of uncertainty or fear. However, living in this world is worth a try rather than being afraid of failure. For instance, I enjoy watching how sailors balance their body on the boat. This maneuver is learned through years of working on a boat and on the sea, especially in the middle of a storm because balance and being adaptable could save your life. Therefore, learning how to adapt your body to the movement of the boat is crucial to keep you on your feet and standing. Being flexible with the current situation and adapting to the natural flow of changing situations allows us to succeed in a new society. For example, when I was studying in Cuba, my ability to accept and to provide critique was minimal based on the political ideologies in Cuba. Initially, it was difficult for me to accept critical criticism given by colleagues due to my conditioned mindset and ideologies of my country of origin. Accepting critique has been part of my ability to adapt while minimizing my level of stress and anxiety without imposing my way of thinking. Kosic refers to Searle and Ward's (1990) psychological adaptation and explains that immigrants who adopt a "strategy of integration" and embrace the "host culture" would encounter less stress in psychological adaptation compared with those who prefer the "strategy of marginalization" (Kosic, 2002).

Despite all the political challenges that the Cuban society and government had to overcome, Cuba is one of the most racially integrated nations in the world. Especially after the 1950's, Fidel's revolutionary objective was to have more access to education and public health. Although the Cuban government was still in control of the economic and Cuban resources, the minority Cuban African descendants have had an opportunity to improve their quality of life and their families through education. The main corporations, health care system, and education is controlled by the government.

This is different when compared to the U.S. Because of the free market philosophy, described by Marc Orlitzky (2019) as " an unregulated system of economic exchange [without government intervention]", the U.S. has become an important economic authority in the world. Therefore, as a new immigrant, you have the opportunity to work as many jobs, projects, and hours as you want. It might empower you to gain different skills and develop different careers at the same time. Although the U.S. has so many opportunities, nationals sometimes do not appreciate or take advantage of this. I believe we need to continue grow ing socially. I cannot conceive how such a resourceful country has such a considerable homeless population living in urban cities. Another social disadvantage is the health care system, especially for immigrants. The country is still debating about what is the best health care system, either as private sector or an opportunity to all people. I believe affordable housing, health care, and education are the primary necessities of all human beings. A society without it will be socially behind.

Additionally, I believe that the U.S. is still racially and socially behind compared to other countries, such as Cuba. Hence, people are still struggling with what it's like to be an American. Are we an American by name only or is there an identity attached to that name? Furthermore we are racially, financially, and culturally divided by zip codes. The zip code dictates resources that are available for you, such as access to a quality education. Consequently, one's experience and status is shaped by factors that may be outside of one's own control.

I consider myself a Cuban African descendant. Although, in Cuba, we are all referred to as Cuban. Here in the U.S., when people see me for the first time, they think I am Afro-American. I noticed that the reaction to an Afro-American is completely different than to a European. For example, an Afro-American will greet you as a fellow comrade even though there is a cultural difference, being that my background is Afro Cuban. During my interactions with the Afro-American culture, I noticed that there are subtle undertones of separation from each other within their own culture, even in the way they speak.

I'm blessed to have many great friends from diverse backgrounds, however on many occasions when an unknown European descendant sees me in a public space, they appear to feel threatened by me as evidenced by a change in their walking pace and shifts to cross the street.

I experienced racism for the first time in Philadelphia; I was on a tour following my check in at the accommodation and three European individuals did not get in the same elevator with me when it had arrived. I am experiencing racism on a day to day basis. Additionally, in 2014, I was living in a beautiful neighborhood in Los Angeles called Alta Dena where I saw the shift in socioeconomic class within the different neighborhoods. I lived in a more Afro-American, Hispanic community and one day a Police officer approached me and asked me whether I had been to jail. "I said no, I haven't been in jail." He said, "Are you sure?" I said I was from Cuba" and he said, "Are you sure." I then responded in Spanish and he responded in Spanish, and I recognized that even though his appearance was European, his background was Mexican American. Ten minutes later, another police officer arrived in his car and was checking my vehicle clearance and noticed that all my documents were in place. They mentioned that they had made a mistake and were looking for someone else. These two experiences made me more aware of how I can be a target in this society because I fit into the American racial stereotypes based on physical appearance rather than getting to know an individual in a more in depth.

Another interesting event took place during my journey here in the U.S. I was visiting my friends in New Mexico. Over the years, they became not only good friends but also part of my family and support system. My friends are of Hispanic descent. They are always ready to help people in need and to serve others. Every time, they treat me like, "Mi casa es su casa" allowing me spend nice vacations in their home. Because of their work, they are busy most of the time and, in return, I reciprocate their service to me by helping them with maintaining their home. One day, early in the morning, I grabbed all the trash and I was on my way to deposit it in a trash container provided by the city. Upon greeting a neighbor that approached, she inquired within seconds, "Are you doing housework for them?" And I replied, "Nope, they are just good friends." I wonder why she would think that I would do housework for my friends? I asked myself, why was she surprised to see me doing an act of kindness for my friends?

I understand that social and racial stereotypes are socially constructed and are a byproduct of American history, however it is possible to write about it and to make a point of how we still have to overcome. I realized as an Afro-Cuban, that there are shifts in the way people connect with me based on the way I articulate myself during conversations. Living in the U.S. after all these years has made me more aware of the importance of understanding society when adapting to a segregated system. It is your decision on how we respond and react to situations and how we can impact others in a way that we are progressing towards a more inclusive society. I hope this book will bring to focus the hidden segregation masked by the individualistic American society. "Keep paying attention, when you no longer believe your conditioned responses you are free to do or not do anything." (Be the Person You Want to Find by Cheri Hub). When we are self-aware of our own subjectivities and privileges, we are more open to take action with options that are available to us.

Persistence

"Man is not fully conditioned and determined but determines himself whether he gives in to conditions or stands up to them."
--- Viktor Frankl

Whether your purpose is pursuing a degree, getting into a business network or buying your dream home, keep persisting until they let you in. Sometimes, people give up when they see that it takes a while to get into a certain type of business, obtaining valuable resources, or getting into any type of long-term commitment. In Cuba, I grew up in an undeserved neighborhood. Our house was made of wood and it started declining due to the severe storms passing by the Caribbean, especially in my area. My mom knew that the best way to get out of that situation was moving to a more affluent community within the Cubans' economy. Every Night, my mother would make a dish and bring it as a gift to one of the city's representatives. Every time, my mother explained to them the difficult situation that we were living in. In spite of some family members and friends who did not understand my mother's persistence; she kept going until one day the representative found a home for our family. Looking back, my mother's perseverance taught me that I must keep persisting and overcome the obstacles and never give up until they let me in.

The Good Side of North America

"Patience is the battleground for now versus later, immediate reward versus delayed gratification, impulsivity versus prudence"
--Stephen S. Hall

Sometimes we focus so much on the problems, that we forget that gratefulness is the doorway to solve them. When I arrived in the U.S., some of the first successful folks I met told me several times, "The limit is in your mind." At the time, I did not understand that statement, but through my journey in this complex and fascinating country, I have learned that regardless of the political, economic, and social climate there is a door that will let you in for the opportunity that you are pursuing.

Learning from everybody you encounter is wise. However, it is wiser to surround yourself with highly successful people. I remember listening to some folks complaining about how difficult it is for Afro-Americans and Latinos to find decent jobs and the lack of opportunities for this group. I cannot deny the African American and Latinos struggles to get into the "mainstream society." However, focusing on the problems and not the solutions creates an endless cycle of disappointment.

Towards this end, America has given us the opportunity to choose our own path by working for an employer or to establish ourselves as individual entrepreneurs where we can transform our ideas into a business that services society. Launching a business is better than having a job. In my experience, sometimes it was better to have a part-time job which allowed me to take ESL classes or earn credits at a Community College that also accepts foreign transcripts via outside resources than to focus on achieving the American dream in a job that you dislike or hate. How about you? Are you more focused on paying your bills or both living simply and investing in your education? The immediacy and time given in taking advantage of the processes in place include accessing resources as I adapted to the "mainstream" society. Remember, your first resource is your time. Why is time your first resource? It is best to invest your time in pursuing your career and establishing a business and skills in order to obtain financial freedom. Although the U.S. stands as a symbol of hope and freedom to be who you want to be and do what you want to do, it is easy for immigrants to find themselves a slave to the economic system.

Take Advantage of Your Time

"Keep improving yourself. Time will pass anyway, and it is better that passes improving yourself than doing nothing"
——Unknown

You can sit and drink a cup of coffee or join the local marathon. Time will pass anyway. In modern times, people pass the time between social media, video games, and other Online entertainment. Unfortunately, reading a good book for many is an old fashioned thing. Books are an account of thoughts, ideas, imaginative fantasies, and past experiences of human beings. Therefore, reading might educate, motivate, and inspire you to become a more well-rounded person. A habit of daily reading might lead you towards your dream profession, job, or business.

Time will pass despite either working towards our dream and a regular job. It would be better to invest in working towards your goals. After I completed my ESL classes in a Community College in Pasadena, California, I was eager to pursue my education. This is why I decided to work five part-time jobs while attending school full-time to pursue my master's degree. I knew that I was incurring debt knowing that I did not have the resources afforded by my family. I knew that as soon as I graduated, I would be able to accomplish my dreams with the opportunity to pay off my student debts. This philosophy in my journey made me unaware of the student debt crisis and financial issues in America, such as getting in debt with insurmountable student loans and using credit without a financial foundation. However, my limited ability to fully understand how the credit system works did not cloud my ability to be grateful that I can still pursue my dreams in this country.

Why is Education Important?

"This lack of self-awareness and intellectual limits can produce some awkward inter-action between experts and laypeople"
----Tom Nichols

Pass on wisdom to the next generation because material wealth might destroy them. We need more thinkers in our society. New entrepreneurs devalue education and praise obtaining wealth through quick Online business opportunities. Financial stability is important towards fulfilling all human necessities. However, the history of human's evolution is connected with thinkers that have been searching for meaning and understanding of all things. They are curious and eager to ask and answer the big questions for the benefit of future generations. I consider my friend Irene Rhodes, who wrote "Colorless, A Spiritual Journey", a thinker of this generation who addresses the things that we all share in common despite our religious beliefs, the color of our skin, ethnicity, and cultural background. I believe her book will revolutionize the future of the American race. I find today that the current generation is distracted with superficial information or interactions rather than developing interpersonal skills and the ability to critically think about the issues in today's society. This is our time; if we do not pay attention to certain issues, such as climate change, homelessness in urban cities, hate among communities, and economic, gender, and class inequality, what will be left for future generations? I wonder if they will be proud of us.

A considerable number of immigrants come from societies where teaching and sharing knowledge goes in one direction, from teacher to student. Especially in totalitarian countries, this produces non-pleasant experiences for those migrating to the U.S. Chamberlain (2009) states that "accepting criticism is not easy, and all of us have been stung by having our work criticized by others" (p. 1029). In the past, during my bachelor's degree in Cuba, I recall that we were listening and asking questions about a specific topic without engaging in a critical debate that allows us to express different points of views. At that time, I believed that everything that I learned was legit without a doubt until I moved to the U.S. and got accepted into a master's degree program.

My first master's degree was in Film Scoring. I was fascinated to know that I could write music for films and television. The difference between a music composer and a film composer is that the music composer usually writes about his/her own feelings or a specific story. The film composer writes for moving pictures.

It is a profession that requires teamwork and a certain understanding of how it is like working with directors, assistants, music editors, orchestrators, sound engineers, and musicians. Therefore, it is crucial to understand criticism as part of the process of perfecting a final product. Chamberlain (2009) points out that "having others criticize your work inevitably improves the end product" (p.1029). In my film scoring class, I was one of eight film composers. Each of us spent long hours writing music for a specific scene of a "classic movie". As an assignment, we had to show the project in class so my classmates could give feedback. In particular, that moment was terrifying for me. Growing up in a different political, economical, and educational system was preventing me from seeing the importance of criticism. There were moments when I thought everybody was against me and my musical ideas. I tried to give positive feedback to my colleagues so they can be benevolent with me the next time. After a long while, I realized that my work developed and grew because of my classmates constructive criticism. So, expect some criticism as part of growing not only professionally but also professionally as a future thinker.

Be an Agent of Change, Not a Victim of Your Present Status

I am aware that this topic might expose some of my own subjectivities. At the time I entered the U.S., the political tensions between the U.S. and Cuba facilitated that Cuban immigrants had some privileges that other South and Central Americans did not have. However, the importance is to recognize those privileges and use them to help other people in need. Agency starts with small deeds. Do not wait until your financial and emotional state improves to help people. Be a blessing whatever you are. Of course, self-care is crucial towards moving forward. Helping other people is part of the process of growing as a human being.

For example, this chapter is inspired by the adversities and endeavors of many undocumented young professionals who were brought to the U.S. as children from South and Central America, called DREAMers. DREAMers, because of their lack of having a social security, are ineligible for financial aid. As a result, they are unable to apply for some accredited universities. However, they managed to work two or three jobs and pay full tuition while striving to obtain a degree from a Community College or University (Fathali, 2013). Despite their immigration status, DREAMers are constantly utilizing their agency to make changes in the current political scene and to help others in need. Furthermore, DREAMers attend rallies demanding equal opportunities and they even created the Unidos Club. This club is a "safe place" that assists undocumented students (Navarro & Estelle-Bazaldua, 2017).

As I write this book, approximately 38,000 unaccompanied children have migrated to the U.S. and are being held in detention centers in Florida and Texas. Most of these minors are coming from Central American countries who are fleeing from drug and gang violence (Crventura, 2014).

Is All This Effort Worth The Struggle?

If at this moment, the only thing you see is darkness, that does not mean that there is no light on the other side. There are three emotional challenges that most immigrants have to overcome. Especially, those who are coming to the U.S. by themselves. Loneliness, feeling homesick, and not meeting your families' expectations are the three main emotional challenges I faced.

Finishing your work and going to an empty home for several years may be an unpleasant experience for many immigrants. Sometimes, I scheduled time to talk to my family in Cuba so I did not have to deal with feeling lonely in those moments. In my experience, I learned that having a set of goals and focusing on my mission could be a good way to channel all emotional challenges into positive outcomes. Positive outcomes could be going to college and getting a degree, owning a house, or launching your own business. Focusing on the positive outcomes will keep focused and overcome those feelings of loneliness, homesickness, and false family expectations.

The best is yet to come, remembering important dates such as birthdays, anniversaries and celebrations can be a very painful experience for many immigrants knowing that you cannot be there to share those experiences while making the sacrifices to remain focused on your purpose. Remaining yourself while you are in this country and remembering why you made the decision to migrate to a new country will keep you focused on your purpose. Many of us have and still struggle when grieving the loss of loved ones in another country without the natural support network to console us in the grieving process. I learned how to remember them the way they were, despite not being there physically with them.

Adapting and co-swishing have been my best ally because it has allowed me to embrace the American culture and learn to celebrate its own events, such as all the national holidays even though they are not part of my own traditions. At times I have forgotten the national holidays in Cuba because I was caught up in the American Dream.

For many immigrants with families living in a first world and developing countries could be a very stressful endeavor. Some family members have the illusion that everybody in the first world is rich. They see the Hollywood movies with expensive houses and cars and they think that is the same way of life for everyone here. Some Cuban-Americans have a developing country mentality and live in a first world country; when visiting Cuba, they drive expensive cars and project a luxurious lifestyle. Because I do not exhibit the same projection as those, some people, including some family members, believe that I am struggling because they do not see that the real investment in educating yourself versus the persona of exhibiting a wealthy appearance.

Do not let loneliness, feeling homesick and family expectations distract you from your goals. It is important to be aware of one's own personal development and growth. If you manage to be successful and reach your goals, in most cases your family will succeed as well.

Measuring my progress yearly, is a good strategy to compare yourself with past years. During my master's degree studies, one of my professors gave me valuable advice. He shared with us that while people were planning to go on vacation or having big parties, he was utilizing that time to check if he accomplished all of his goals and compared his progress with previous years.

In conclusion, an immigrant's transition into the U.S. is riddled with challenges or obstacles and also opportunities for personal growth and professional development. Navigating a new environment is naturally filled with uncertainty and doubt. Find the motivation to accomplish any short and long-term goals while in the U.S. Having questions, fears, and disappointment is a normal part of the journey of immigrating to the U.S., but it does not have to be defined in these terms. Alternatively, this journey can be defined by self-growth, hope, and inspiration, either for yourself or others. Everyone can achieve success if provided with the appropriate support, resources, and guidance. This book's purpose is designed to be a personal resource that any immigrant, or anyone for that matter, can turn to when "times get rough" or you feel that you are simply at a "dead end." May this provide the guidance and support that you are searching for.

Will you leave a book review?

Share any insight you learned from this book. Your story might inspire others if you post a short review! Your support and suggestions will improve my future publications.
To leave a review, go here:
http://www.josielperez.com/index.html

Glossary of Terms

Assimilation- An immigrant assimilation strategy that is the partial or total rejection of an immigrants culture of origin and the full adoption of U.S. culture. [The absorption of a minority group into a majority population, during which the group takes on the values and norms of the dominant culture.]

Born-Again Person- The author uses this analogy to describe a new beginning for an immigrant in a new country.

Co-switching- McWilliams (2018), defines co-switching as an act of altering how you express yourself based on your audience.

Integration- An immigrant assimilation strategy that is a merge between one's culture of origin and U.S. culture. [A function that has an integral….]

Marginalization- An immigrant assimilation strategy that is a partial or total rejection of U.S. culture and full adoption of the immigrants culture of origin. [A treatment of a person, group, or concept as insignificant or peripheral.]

Metamorphosis- The transformation from larval to adult form. In Drosophila the destruction of larval tissues and their replacement with adult ones is triggered by 20-hydroxy-ecdysone.

Visualization- A form of meditation where an image of a Buddha or some other divine being is creatively imagined for purposes of devotion or spiritual transformation

Appendix A: List of Resources

The Arizona Language Center (www.arizonalanguagecenter.com)
A2Z Evaluations (www.a2zeval.com)
Friendly House (www.friendlyhouse.org)
Josiel Perez (Josielperez.com)

References

Bammer, A. (Ed.). (1994). Displacements: Cultural identities in question. Indiana University Press.

Berry, J. W. (1997). Lead Article - Immigration, Acculturation, and Adaptation. Applied Psychology, 46(1), 5-34. doi:10.1080/026999497378467

Bishop, C. D., Erezyilmaz, D. F., Flatt, T., Georgiou, C. D., Hadfield, M. G., Heyland, A., ... & Reitzel, A. M. (2006). What is metamorphosis?. Integrative and Comparative Biology, 46(6), 655-661.

Chamberlain, M. (2009). The Importance of Criticism and of Keeping it in Perspective. Journal of Wildlife Management, 73(7), 1029-1030.

Crventura. (2014). Treatment of Unaccompanied Minors in Detention Centers. Retrieved July 23, 2019, from http://pages.vassar.edu/children-of-immigration/2014/12/15/treatment-of-unaccompa-nied-minors-in-detention-centers/

Fathali, H. (2013). The American DREAM: DACA, DREAMers, and comprehensive immigration re-form. Seattle UL Rev., 37, 221.

Frankl, V.E. (2006). Man's search for meaning. Boston, MA: Beacon Press.

Green, J. (2010). Dictionary. Green's Dictionary of Slang, Green's Dictionary of Slang

Hanna, A. V., & Ortega, D. M. (2014). Salir adelante (perseverance): Lessons from the Mexican immigrant experience. Journal of Social Work, 16(1), 47-65. doi:10.1177/1468017314560301

Kosic, A. (2002). Acculturation Attitudes, Need for Cognitive Closure, and Adaptation of Immigrants. The Journal of Social Psychology, 142(2), 179-201. doi:10.1080/00224540209603894

McWilliams, AT (2018, July 25). Sorry to Bother You, black Americans and the power and peril of code-switching. The Guardian. Retrieved from https://www.theguardian.com/film/2018/jul/25/sorry-to-bother-you-white-voice-code-switching

Mahalingam, R. (2013). Cultural psychology of immigrants: An introduction. In Cultural psychology of immigrants (pp. 17-28). Psychology Press.

Mattoo, A., Neagu, I. C., & Ozden, C. (2005). Brain waste? Educated immigrants in the US labor market. The World Bank.

Marc Orlitzky. (2019). Free market. Britannica Online Academic Edition, Encyclopædia Britannica, Inc.

Navarro, J., & Estelle-Bazaldua, S. (2017). DREAMers Awareness Project.

Nichols, T. M. (2019). The death of expertise: The campaign against established knowledge and why it matters. New York, NY: Oxford University Press.

Nilep, C. (2006). "Code switching" in sociocultural linguistics. Colorado Research in Linguistics, 19(1), 1.

Steiner, L., & Schneider, L. (2013). The happy artist: an empirical application of the work-preference model. Journal of Cultural Economics, 37(2), 225-246.

Suddendorf, T., Oostenbroek, J., Nielsen, M., & Slaughter, V. (2012). Is newborn imitation developmentally homologous to later social-cognitive skills? Developmental Psychobiology, 55(1), 52-58. doi:10.1002/dev.21005

Summary

Immigrants who immigrate to another country have rich histories and previous lives that they carry with them upon an establishment of a new life, such as into the United States. However, many obstacles could be presented along this journey that can impact a transition, such as cultural differences, familial relations, and language difficulties. Also, there can be lots of uncertainty around navigating an unfamiliar environment. Finding the motivation and courage to accomplish any established short and long-term goals while in the United States is a challenge that many immigrants face. Having questions, fears, and disappointment is a normal part of the journey of immigrating to the United States, but it does not have to be defined in these terms. Alternatively, this journey can be defined by self-growth, hope, and inspiration, either for yourself or others. Everyone can achieve success if provided with the appropriate support, resources, and guidance. This book's purpose is designed to be a personal resource that any immigrant, or anyone for that matter, can turn to when "times get rough" or you feel that you are simply at a "dead end." May this provide the guidance and support that you are searching for.

9 781697 688221